Finding Faith Through My Father's Stroke

A Journey of Faith, Fear, and Miracles

By Amanda Southard

Finding Faith Through My Father's Stoke

A Journey of Faith, Fear, and Miracles

Published in 2025 by Broken Yoke Publishing, LLC.
BrokenYokePublishing.com

Broken Yoke Publishing
3080 I-70 Business Loop
Grand Junction, CO 81504

www.BrokenYokePublishing.com

ISBN: 978-1-955941-49-5

DEDICATION

Special thanks to:

Salim Ghorayeb PA

Dr. Edward Maurin

Dr. Eric Momin

Dr. Jonathan Belk

Dr. Seth Kareus

Thank you for taking such good care of my dad and for always being there to answer questions for us. Thank you for answering my questions while I was doing my research for this book.

This book is dedicated to my daddy, Eric Kincade.

FOREWORD

In 2023, my dad had a stroke. The months that followed left our family feeling lost, afraid, and at times, very alone.

By Christmas of 2024, I was sitting on the couch scrolling through Amazon, trying to find gifts for my family, when an idea came to me: Why not get my dad a daily devotional for the new year? Surely that would help strengthen his faith and rekindle the fire I knew was still there in his heart.

Excited, I began searching. First I typed: "Devotionals for stroke survivors." Nothing. Then: "Devotionals for head injury." Nothing. One last try: "Devotionals for head trauma." Still nothing.

The results that did appear were mostly about addiction, depression, or anxiety—important topics, yes, but none of them spoke directly to what my dad was going through.

And then it hit me: Why not write one myself?

This lit a fire in my soul like never before. Writing notes and letters to my dad had been a trademark of our relationship since I was a little girl. I used to scribble little letters and tuck them into the screen door so he would find them on his way out to work. I wouldn't be surprised if he still has some of those stashed away.

In that moment, I could almost audibly hear the Lord speak to me:

"I am trying to reach him, but he isn't hearing Me. I need you to deliver My message to him."

I immediately reached out to my pastor and to a friend from church whom I believed worked with a small publishing company and had been published herself. To my surprise, when we met at her office, I discovered she didn't just work at a publishing company—she owned one.

We talked about my vision for this devotional, we prayed over it, and I confessed how overwhelmed I felt by the task God was giving me. But then I remembered Philippians 4:6–7:

"Do not be anxious about anything, but in every situation, by prayer and petition, with thanksgiving, present your requests to God. And the peace of God, which transcends all understanding, will guard your hearts and your minds in Christ Jesus."

So that's exactly what I did.

As the words began to flow, something unexpected happened: I began to feel healing for myself. Piece by piece, God lifted the weight from my heart.

This devotional is first and foremost for my dad. But my prayer is that if even one other person picks it up and finds hope, peace, or healing through these words, then it has served its purpose.

Prayer:

Heavenly Father, bless my hands as I write these words. Let them be a vessel for Your message and Your peace. May these pages reflect not my voice, but Yours. In Jesus' name, Amen.

Isaiah 41:10

"So do not fear, for I am with you.
Do not be dismayed, for I am your God.
I will strengthen you and help you.
I will uphold you with my righteous right hand."

WEEK 1

God's Presence in Chaos

Learning to let God hold me

It was just another Tuesday. Patients in and out of the busy neurology clinic. The physician's assistant, Salim, directing me to call primary care doctors with alerts of high blood pressures, Dr. Witwer's hair pointing in all directions. Then I got the call.

"Daddy had a stroke. They're rushing him to St. Mary's in an ambulance now."

It felt like a curtain fell on a lit stage. How could this have happened? He's only forty-seven years old, for goodness' sake! I went straight to Salim. He pulled up the imaging and showed me where it had occurred, the right side of his cerebellum, at the brain stem. I was scared. But I had to hold it together. I was at work. I'm the oldest daughter. I'm the strong one. There's no time for fear when others depend on you to be strong, right?

Even at twenty-seven years old, I still felt like a little girl that just needed her daddy. The soul crushing fear of losing him crashed over me.

We later found out that medically speaking, my dad was lucky to be alive. He had gone more than twelve hours without medical intervention. I know it's not luck, but a miracle from God. In that dark moment of fear, God heard my cry for help.

"Lord please, don't let me lose my daddy. I can't do life without him. Keep me strong for my brothers, my stepmom, my daughter, and most importantly, for him."

God wrapped me in His arms and said, "Breathe. Trust in me. I will strengthen you. I will lift you up. I am with you."

I didn't move forward without tears, but I did move forward with confidence. No matter what happened, I was certain that my dad's life, and mine, were in God's hands.

My dad had a long road of recovery ahead of him, but I knew God would deliver him.

Today's Prayer

Heavenly Father, thank You for Your almighty protection. Thank You for being good, and faithful, and consistent. Thank You for Your peace. We ask that going forward You continue to wash over us with peace, healing, and most importantly, gratitude. Gratitude for our day to day, for our continued life, and Your continued presence. In Jesus name, amen.

Reflection Questions:

Where in your life do you feel the need to "hold it together"?

How might God be inviting you to let Him hold *you* instead?

Journal your experience here

Joshua 1:9

"Have I not commanded you?
Be strong and courageous. Do not be frightened,
and do not be dismayed, for the Lord your God is with you
wherever you go."

WEEK 2

Listening to God Over Fear

Silencing the lies, hearing His voice

Recovery from a stroke is a roller coaster, not just for the patient but for the family. My dad's strongest emotion during those first months was anger. He lashed out, sometimes saying he was upset with us for "holding on to him instead of letting him go to Jesus."

Knowing my dad the way that I do, I knew that his anger was rooted in fear, sadness, and feelings of hopelessness, but that didn't make it any easier to watch. The strongest man I knew wanted to give up. Anxiety gripped me. What if he did?

I wasn't listening to the Lord. I was listening to my anxieties. I was letting Satan whisper in my ear. "You're going to lose him. He isn't going to make it. Your daughter will forget her Pop-Pop. God is failing you."

These thoughts consumed me. My husband was increasingly worried about my well-being as I turned away from God, and toward alcohol. My days were filled with caregiving, work, parenting, and trying to be a good wife, but I wasn't caring for my own soul. My Bible collected dust. My craft table sat untouched. At church, my body was present. But my heart was numb. I even stopped praying with my daughter.

Then one day, God broke through the noise. "Why aren't you hearing me? You're seeking comfort in the wrong places. You know I am the answer. Why are you angry with me?"

I had no answer, but I knew He was right. I sat down, prayed, and picked up a craft project. At that moment, I felt a small but significant shift. Sometimes, the bravest thing we can do is pause, listen, and let Him realign us.

Today's Prayer:

Heavenly Father, please continue to remind us of the importance of LISTENING to You. Remind us to place our fears at Your feet, so that You can absorb them and squash them. There is no peace but in Your presence. In Jesus name, amen.

Reflection Questions:

What voices or distractions are louder than God in your life right now?

What is one small way you can pause and listen for Him this week?

Journal your experience here

Matthew 9:20-22

"Just then, a woman who had been subject to bleeding for twelve years came up behind him and touched the edge of his cloak. She said to herself, 'If I only touch his cloak, I will be healed.' Jesus turned and saw her. 'Take heart, daughter,' He said, 'your faith has healed you.'
And the woman was healed at that moment."

WEEK 3

A Miracle with Water

Prayers answered in unexpected ways

According to Stroke.org, strokes occur when a blood vessel carrying important nutrients and oxygen to the brain is blocked or ruptured. The most important thing when a stroke occurs is time. The quicker medical intervention happens, the better chance of a full recovery.

Cerebellum strokes, specifically, have a very high mortality rate. They are rare, and account for less than ten percent of all strokes. Complications include coordination issues, difficulties with balance, and dizziness, as the cerebellum is the part of the brain responsible for these functions.

Strokes that occur in the brain stem only occur about ten percent of the time as well, and only have a survival rate of about thirty percent. These types of strokes cause difficulty swallowing, breathing problems, vision issues, motor control difficulties, loss of sensation, coma, and in severe cases "locked-in syndrome". This is where the body is paralyzed except for eye movement, essentially leaving the person conscious but unable to communicate or move.

My dad had several of these complications. During the first difficult weeks, he struggled the most with the inability to swallow. He had a G-tube placed, which is a tube sticking out of the stomach in which formula, water, and medications can be poured directly into the stomach, bypassing the esophagus. The speech therapist at the hospital told us that she rarely saw the ability to swallow return in less than a year. If at all. I began to pray every night and day.

"God, please. Heal his throat. If he can swallow again, he'll regain his hope. Please, Lord."

On day thirty, a trickle of water slid down his throat, and with it a tear slid down my dad's cheek. Our prayer had been answered.

Today's Prayer:

Heavenly Father, You are the Almighty Deliverer. Your hand alone heals the sick and broken. I know with every ounce of my being that You will take what hurts and what's broken in me and heal me. Thank You, Heavenly Father, for Your healing power. In Jesus name, amen.

Reflection Questions:

Find a quiet time once a day for the next week. Pray specifically over the area you most need healing, and truly believe that God will deliver.

Journal your experience here

Hebrews 12:2

"Fixing our eyes on Jesus, the author and perfecter of faith,
who for the joy set before Him endured the cross,
scorning its shame, and sat down
at the right hand of the throne of God."

WEEK 4

Refocusing on Jesus

Finding my anchor when life feels like it's spinning

A week after my dad was able to swallow that trickle of water, we hosted my daughter's second birthday party at the local trampoline park. We got pizza and donuts. There was a huge crowd, terrible lighting, lots of noise, and seating consisted of picnic tables with benches. I talked with my stepmom beforehand, explaining that we would completely understand if my dad was not up to attending. But he INSISTED on being at the party. He was not going to miss his only grandchild's second birthday. The day arrived, and he sat for the forty-minute drive, got out of the car, and stumbled his way across the uneven parking lot into the building. He choked down a donut and a piece of pizza, and did his best to interact with his over excited two-year-old granddaughter who wanted nothing more than for Pop-Pop to come jump with her.

He may have regained his ability to swallow, but his migraines were still unbearable, and his dizziness was nauseating.

The physical therapist taped brightly colored squares of paper in different spots around the house. This exercise helped Dad focus on anchor points, and helped him quite literally, not spin out of control.

This visual exercise is actually a great spiritual exercise as well. When life feels out of control and dizzying due to our physical circumstances, we need to remember to focus on JESUS to center ourselves.

While Jesus was on the cross, he cried out to his father "My God, my God, why have you forsaken me?" This exact thought plagued my dad. He felt as though he had been abandoned by his Heavenly Father. Life can feel scary and uncertain at many points. Now add in a traumatic brain injury due to a life altering stroke. He was scared, confused, not sure if he'd ever be the same. He was feeling all of these feelings and many more.

My dad needed to realign and make Jesus the center of his focus, much like those brightly colored squares of paper all over the house. Jesus was abused on that cross, for the purpose of fulfilling prophecy that had been set by our Heavenly Father, the King of Kings, long before Jesus was born on the earth. We may not know or understand the reasons that our suffering occurs, but if we remember that we are in the hands of an almighty, and all LOVING Father, then that suffering may seem insignificant to the greater outcome.

We may question God on why these things are happening to us, and that's great. God loves our questions. He wants us to turn to Him. He also hopes that we turn these things into something that can be used by Him. He has a reason and a purpose for us, even if we can't see it.

Today's Prayer:

Heavenly Father, forgive me for forgetting that You are always there and that You are all-knowing. Your plan is greater than anything I could ever know. Help me to refocus on You in my times of distress and turmoil as well as in my times of peace. In Jesus name, amen.

Reflection Questions:

What "anchors" help you refocus on Jesus when life feels overwhelming?

How might your current trial be used for God's greater purpose?

Journal your experience here

2 Corinthians 5:7

"Therefore we are always confident
and know that as long as we are at home in the body
we are away from the Lord.
For we walk by faith not by sight."

WEEK 5

Walking by Faith

Choosing trust over fear

Christmas. A time spent joyously gathering and celebrating with loved ones. This Christmas was even more significant than most. We had come so close to this being a time of grief rather than celebration. My dad had progressed from his walker to his cane for ambulation, which I didn't even know until Christmas Eve.

Dad was excited for this Christmas. When we arrived at his home, he met us outside and took my daughter, Adelaide, by the hand. He had her inside with a sweet treat in her little fist before we even had the car doors closed. This made me happy, but also sad. He was still very thin and unsteady. The squares for his PT were posted all around the house. Adelaide spent most of the day obsessing over the yellow one that was at her eye level. She wanted to play with Pop-Pop's "colors ball" as she called it.

The day was full of joy. We called my grandpa, and he talked us through the process of making the secret family fruit salad recipe. We watched *A Christmas Story*, quoting lines at each other. We unwrapped gifts, gushing over Adelaide's presents. But there was still a cloud over our family.

Dad was doing his best to be engaged and act festive. He was right behind Adelaide every step of the way. They played with her new toys and went for long walks around the rugged terrain of the property. He played the typical dad on Christmas morning, picking up the wrapping paper trash. He ate a considerable amount of fruit salad, as it was soft and easy on his weakened esophagus.

I could see, though. I could see how dizzy he was every time he bent down to pick up the discarded wrapping paper. I could see how hard it was for him to navigate around the holes in the ground and the rocks that we took for granted as the normal path. I could see him wince as he swallowed every bite. I was anxious and worried whenever he stumbled. I tried to insist he use his walker, that he sit down and relax. He refused all of it.

You see, I was letting satan whisper in my ear that Dad wasn't ready, that he was going to hurt himself, and it would be the straw that broke the camel's back.

My dad, however, was walking by faith. He was allowing the Lord to guide his steps not only physically, but spiritually. He was being the man he had been my entire life – the man who put his faith in his Heavenly Father, and not in those around him who were filled with fear.

Today's Prayer:

Heavenly Father, please guide my feet, not only physically but spiritually, as I chase my healing ambitions. Please help me to be confident in You and Your power. In Jesus name, amen.

Reflection Questions:

Where in your life do you need to step forward in faith even if the ground feels unsteady?

How might walking by faith bring you closer to God's promises?

Journal your experience here

Psalm 4:8

"In peace I will both lie down and sleep;
for you alone, O Lord, make me dwell in safety"

WEEK 6

Resting in the Lord's safety

Healing with rest

New Year's Day. We made it through the dreadful events of the previous year, and were determined to look forward with hope. The fact that we almost lost my dad loomed over us. We cherished every moment with him now.

The thing about stroke is that the risk of a second stroke within the first year is very high. It is also less likely to see further improvement in basic function or symptomatology after the initial six months. And so, without realizing, we set an imaginary deadline: Daddy had to be fully healed by April of the next year.

But healing is unique. No two journeys look the same. For my dad, his healing looked like a lot of sleep. Before his stroke, he battled terrible insomnia, sometimes staying awake for days on end. When we suddenly saw him sleeping so much, we worried. Was this healing, or was he declining?

I consulted with my friend Salim, a Physician's Assistant for Neurosurgery. He assured me that sleeping was exactly what my dad needed. Poor Salim had to deal with a lot of frantic phone calls from me in those first six months.

"Remember Amanda, your father has had a traumatic injury to his brain. The thing his brain needs to heal now is rest."

While my dad was resting physically, my stepmom and I were learning how to rest spiritually. We gave ourselves permission to cry together, to encourage each other, and to let God hold us in our weariness. Around that time, I stopped drinking, and poured my energy into my work. My stepmom began reading her Bible again.

In resting with the Lord and dwelling in His safety, something shifted. Slowly, passion began to return, not only for our work and hobbies, but for Him.

Today's Prayer:

Heavenly Father, please help me to feel safe in rest. Remind me that without rest, I cannot accomplish the goals You have set for me. In Jesus name, amen.

Reflection Questions:

In what areas of life do you struggle to trust God enough to rest, and how can you release those fears to Him?

How has God used rest, whether physical, emotional, or spiritual, to bring healing or renewal in your own journey?

Journal your experience here

Proverbs 18:22

"He who finds a wife finds a good thing and obtains favor from the Lord."

WEEK 7

Embodying Christ

Choosing love every day

Sometimes, when the unthinkable happens, the Lord calls us to step up in ways we never thought possible. A call to action from the Almighty, so to speak. When that time came for my family, my step- mom took that call to action with strength and grace. She married my dad when I was just six years old, and immediately showered me in love. She stepped in and became the wife my dad needed, and the bonus mom that every little girl in my position wanted. Evil stepmom? Not in my family.

The first couple of months after Dad's stroke, he lashed out often. Traumatic brain injuries like stroke often affect the prefrontal cortex, which is the part of the brain that controls anger responses and aggression. Psychology tells us the person you are closest to is the person who sees the worst side of you, and in this case that happened to be true. My stepmom was the one he lashed out at the most as she was the one with him 24/7.

She had every right to be angry, upset, snap back. She could have responded with impatience or frustration. But she didn't. She woke up every day and actively chose love in moments where many would have chosen to walk away.

My stepmom scheduled appointments, had remodels done to the bathroom to make the shower safer, researched stroke and how to support loved ones during times of crisis. She prayed for recovery for my dad. She prayed for strength for herself. Not only was she caring for my dad at this time, she was serving the Lord through her actions.

She continued to be the woman and role model that I had grown up admiring. My stepmom demonstrated the kind of loving wife described in the Bible. She was Sarah to Abraham.

Jesus tells us as women many times throughout the Bible to serve our husbands as well as stating that men should protect and care for their wives. We are called to love our spouses and in doing so we are called to care for our spouses in their most fragile and vulnerable state.

Today's Prayer:

Heavenly Father, bless the wives of the world who are stepping up and embodying You through their actions with their families. Bless their hearts and give them the strength they need to care for their loved ones in their greatest times of need. In Jesus name, amen.

Reflection Questions:

How can you embody the image that Christ has for you?

How can you serve your loved ones this week?

Journal your experience here

John 14:27

"Peace I leave with you; my peace I give you.
I do not give to you as the world gives.
Do not let your hearts be troubled and do not be afraid."

WEEK 8

Peace In His Presence

Feeling His embrace

February came around and Dad was doing better. No longer using his walker, and rarely needing his cane, he was able to eat most things again without difficulty. He was still sleeping a lot but not as much as he was initially. Dad and my stepmom decided that a vacation would be beneficial, so off they went on a tropical cruise to St. Martins in the Bahamas.

Looking at the pictures of the trip I couldn't help but think that they both looked so at peace. It was almost as though the Lord himself was wrapping his arms around the couple and breathing new life into them. I don't think I had ever seen them so relaxed and happy.

When Dad got home, scorched from the sun, he shared that while he was in the water, just floating, he felt almost normal again. He had felt the Lord's presence embracing him and healing him through the water. His face lit up with a huge smile. It was the first real smile I'd seen from him since his stroke. I was so happy, that I cried.

The Lord provided us the perfect sanctuary in which to lose our anxieties and truly connect with him. Jesus Himself retreated into the wilderness to connect with the Holy Father and I firmly believe that we should follow that example in times of anxiety and stress. Even though I wasn't able to accompany them on this trip, I spent time by the nearby river, praying by the water and listening to His voice through the wind. It genuinely healed a small part of my soul.

Today's Prayer:

Heavenly Father, thank You for providing us with this beautiful planet. Thank You for speaking to us through the trees, the water, and the wind. Thank You for Your warm embrace in times of cold fear. Please continue to bless us in these ways, and continue to heal us through Your love. In Jesus name, amen.

Reflection Questions:

When was the last time you felt God's peace in a way that calmed your heart and reminded you of His presence?

How can you intentionally seek out quiet moments, whether in nature, prayer, or stillness, to let the Lord's embrace refresh your soul?

Journal your experience here

Ecclesiastes 3:11

"He has made everything beautiful in its time.
He has also set eternity in the human heart;
yet no one can fathom what God has done from beginning to end."

WEEK 9

Trusting the Lord's Timeline

Holding space for ups and downs

After almost losing his life, my dad decided to cherish every moment and live life to the fullest. He wanted to see the world and he felt that cruises would be the most effective way to do so. He also felt that after doing so well on the tropical cruise he would be able to handle another one with ease. He and my stepmom embarked on a Canadian cruise out of New York.

This time though, Dad realized he was still going to have ups as well as downs. He came home from this cruise struggling. Dizziness had increased, the headaches came back with a vengeance, and he struggled with eating on the cruise. We were all concerned that he'd had another stroke.

After a consult with his neurologist, it was determined that Dad just pushed himself too hard. He had always been that way. When I was growing up, he worked forty hours a week in 120-degree weather as a bee keeper, and then another thirty hours a week at night, moving those bees to pollinate the fields around our valley. On the weekends he would spend all day Saturday doing yard work and renovating the house and then he would spend Sundays in church and resting up to do it all over again. He didn't know how to take it easy. He was famous for saying "if you're not fifteen minutes early you're late" and "if you're going to do something do it right and give it your all."

Something that can be hard to understand about our bodies is that if we do not allow our bodies to rest, our bodies will MAKE us rest. After his stroke, Dad was learning this lesson the hard way. He was trying to live as if he'd never had the stroke. In some ways this was great, but he also needed to understand that because of this traumatic experience, he now must learn to take the bad with the good. Dad needed to learn to trust the Lord's process and timeline for his healing.

Being a man of action, Dad was ready to jump right back into life as he knew it. But God's timeline doesn't always align with what we think it should be. The almighty Lord works in mysterious ways. We know that my dad was lucky to be alive. Dad spent his whole life working hard to provide for his family. Now it was his family's turn to take care of him, and allow him the safety to rest.

Today's Prayer:

Heavenly Father, please remind me to hold space for the ups and downs of life. Remind me to trust Your timeline and to be thankful for the breath of life You breathe into me every day. In Jesus name, amen.

Reflection Questions:

In what areas of your life are you tempted to rush ahead instead of waiting on God's timing?

How can you remind yourself to embrace both the ups and downs as part of God's plan for your growth and healing?

Journal your experience here

Ezekiel 36:26

"I will give you a new heart and put a new spirit within you; and I will remove the heart of stone from your flesh and give you a heart of flesh."

WEEK 10

Feeling the Spirit

Settling into the new normal

It's been more than six months. They say that at the six-month mark, you've hit the point of healing that you are going to reach. My dad was able to eat and drink normally again. He was still very dizzy and suffered from constant headaches, but he was trying to learn to manage. Through physical therapy, Dad discovered that he did well on the balance board that resembled a skateboard. This re-ignited a passion for skateboarding that he had possessed as a kid and young adult.

Some of my fondest memories of childhood were when Dad would take my brothers and I to the skatepark. We would listen to skate music and play while he hit the ramps. These were rare moments that Dad was able to let loose and have fun, and he loved sharing it with his kids.

Dad began to settle into his new routine of life. He purchased skateboards and practiced his balance in the house by holding onto the walls and skating around the kitchen. Sometimes, on a good day, he'd take one to the skatepark and attempt to go without assisting devices. He even bought my daughter, my husband, and my brothers new skateboards for Christmas. Seeing the excitement on his face warmed my heart. It was like looking into the past, when I was a kid and he gave me my first skateboard.

The Lord was truly working a miracle in Dad's heart, removing the anger, or the heart of stone, and breathing new life into him. The Lord was igniting a fire of excitement where there had only been grief and sadness before. It was an amazing thing to witness.

Even though Dad had to adjust to a "new normal" so to speak, he was finding new and old passions that helped him move away from grief, anger, and sadness. It was a reminder that I also need to pour my energy into healthy activities and coping mechanisms.

Today's Prayer:

Heavenly Father, thank You for igniting passions in our hearts for You. Thank You for providing us with healthy coping skills and healthy alternatives to what satan tries to fill our hearts with. Thank You for being the Almighty Deliverer and Loving Father. In Jesus name, amen.

Reflection Questions:

Where in your life has God replaced heaviness, anger, or grief with new passions, joy, or peace?

What healthy coping skills or passions can you lean into right now to draw closer to God and strengthen your heart?

Journal your experience here

Author's note:

Thank you so much for reading this devotional. This was very healing for me to write and I hope that it helped heal a part of you as well. My goal was to help as many people as possible feel that there is hope after a stroke. There are always ups and downs after a stroke and it is very rare that people go back to life as they knew it prior to that event, but through the Lord Almighty, anything is possible.

This started out as a Devotional dedicated to helping stroke survivors find hope, but it ended up being more about watching my loved one navigate life after stroke, and dealing with those feelings and fears. I felt incredible relief as I wrote and I hope that this is conveyed in the writing.

I'd like to close with a prayer,

Heavenly Father,

Thank You for working miracles in our lives on a daily basis – even if we don't realize it. You are always there and always working for our benefit. You are an amazing, wonderful, all-powerful God, and without You none of this would be possible. Thank You for allowing me the opportunity to share my story, and for letting it find the person reading this. May they feel Your presence in these writings. In Jesus name, amen.

About the Author

Amanda Southard is a Christian whose faith was forged in fire during one of life's darkest valleys. As a specialized medical assistant in neurosurgery, she experienced both sides of the trauma room when her father suffered a massive stroke—one that should have ended his life but instead became a powerful testimony of God's miraculous intervention.

Walking through her father's recovery transformed Amanda's understanding of hope, healing, and divine faithfulness. That journey inspired her to write this devotional for stroke survivors and the families who stand beside them in the long road ahead.

Amanda lives with her husband and daughter, grateful daily for their unwavering love and support. Through these pages, she hopes to offer the comfort, encouragement, and Christ-centered hope that sustained her family when medical odds weren't enough.

LOOK FOR THESE GREAT BOOKS FROM
BROKEN YOKE PUBLISHING

Exclusive North American distributor of

The World English Bible

Rocky Mountain Medley Novella Collection

Uranium Downs by Jessica Bertrand

Interruption by Robin Densmore Fuson

The Orchard's Secret *by Templa Melnick*

Price of Grace by Debra Shelton

Books by Templa Melnick

Season of Forgiveness

Season of Redemption

Books by Jessica Bertrand

Dinosaurs, Assassins, and Monarchs

Purloined in Paris

Books by Darlene Welsh

Priceless Moments: Lessons From Our Grandchildren

Priceless Moments 2: Lessons From Our Grandchildren

Books by Chris Melnick

The Messianic Passover Celebration

www.ingramcontent.com/pod-product-compliance
Lightning Source LLC
LaVergne TN
LVHW051021080826
845145LV00009B/2744

* 9 7 8 1 9 5 5 9 4 1 4 9 5 *